ON VICTORY OF MR. DONALD TRUMP

Realizing Prosperity and Justice in America and the World

RYUHO OKAWA

HS Press

Original title: "Trump Shin Daitoryo De Sekai Wa Ko Ugoku"

HS Press is an imprint of IRH Press Co., Ltd.
Tokyo
ISBN 13: 979-8-88737-086-6
Interior Image: AFP=JIJI
First Edition (updated)

Contents

Q&A

Preface

This is "what I believe."
America is still alive.
America should be America.
America should be a great and strong teacher.
The result shows God's will.
Now is the time to believe.
The victory of Mr. Donald Trump is the answer.
He will rebuild the United States greater again.
I hope so. We hope so. People of the world hope so.
This is the correct answer.
America shall not be divided again.

Nov. 11, 2016
Master and CEO of Happy Science Group
Ryuho Okawa

1

Guardian spirit already said, "I will be the next president" In January of this year

Yesterday, we recognized the conclusion of the presidential race of the United States, and as you know, Donald Trump won [see Figure 1]. It's very

Figure 1.
On the early morning of November 9, 2016, the president-elect Donald Trump gave his victory speech in New York.

happy for us because we did "a little" for Mr. Trump. My cuffs button, this is not so precious one, but he gave me these cuffs in respect for my New York mission.[*] So, I appreciated him and he also appreciated me. We are Avengers[†], so we can respect each other.

Early this year, in January, I published the spiritual message from the guardian spirit of Donald Trump [see Figure 2]. In that book, he already said, "I'm not the frontrunner of the presidency. I will be the next president." He repeatedly said so. And

Figure 2.
Ryuho Okawa, *The Trump Secret* (New York: IRH Press, 2017).

For more on spiritual message and guardian spirit, see end section.

---

[*] On October 2nd, 2016, Master Ryuho Okawa gave a lecture in English, "Freedom, Justice, and Happiness" at Crowne Plaza Times Square Manhattan in New York.

[†] A piece featuring a team of various American comic book heroes. A film was made in 2012 which was considered a big hit, and a sequel was released in 2015.

this was not a joke. He became president, as you know. This is his confidence, I think so.

But at the time, audience might have thought that it was his joke because he said at the time that he's the rebirth of George Washington, the founder of the United States and he said, "I will be the next president." So, the audience might have felt that he's just joking, or as always, he said that he talks a lot about him, bigger than he is.

But in reality, he said the truth and in that conversation, our Miss Isis Mariko talked about him that he's an honest man and he thought that it's very suitable for him. And I visited this October and gave a lecture at New York's hotel and I repeatedly said he's an honest man and reliable man and responsible man. This is my honest opinion of him.

2

His victory comes from his strategy And God's wind from Heaven

To tell the truth, American mass media and Japanese mass media and, of course, a lot of intelligent people who can speak a lot about him by writing or by speaking through the media didn't think his victory. But I continuously insisted that he deserves to be the next president. He has such kind of capacity and reliability as the next president of the United States. But American scholars and journalists couldn't understand what I said because Donald Trump is very difficult to understand from the outside.

He, himself, has new weapon for new age. This is the weapon through his mouth, I mean, the radical words, radical and creative words. Sometimes it sounds very extreme, and sometimes he was told that he is accustomed to make sexual harassment or racial harassment, like that. But I think that he indeed is a gentleman and he sometimes acts like Mr. Duterte of the Philippines, but in reality, he is not such kind of type. He is a very intelligent and wise person, and he has calculations for the reaction of the mass media.

And I guessed that he will win, this summer, because Mr. Trump let the media dance at his will. When we read newspapers from America or we watched TV of the American news, Mr. Trump appeared twice as many times as Ms. Clinton. It is a strategy, I think so. He is very wise, clever. His money for running the presidency was smaller than Ms. Clinton's money and also, his moving mates for presidency had been fewer than Hillary's. But he finally won.

In reality, when we watched the TV yesterday, we felt some kind of so-called *kamikaze*, the wind of god, from Heaven. The real difference of the number of the votes is about one million or so*.

* The total popular vote as of 2 pm on Nov. 11 (JST), the day after this lecture, was roughly 60.05 million for Trump and 60.44 million for Clinton.

Of course, Mr. Trump won against Ms. Clinton, but almost one million. But he got a great victory. It comes from his strategy, I think so. People of the world know Donald Trump very much in this year. His strategy of the propaganda was very systematic and reasonable.

So, it's a very good sample even for us in Japan to deal with political activity of Japan. If the mass media predict the result of the election, it always holds true. But in America, as you just watched several or ten or more hours ago, the result could change.

I think this is one aspect of democracy. People who have the right for voting can choose by their own, or his own or her own, thinking. Just on their own mind, not on the tendency of the mass media or intelligent people or casters or famous scholars. They hear from them, but they judge by themselves and they change their mind in these two or three days, I guess so. This is, from one aspect is, kamikaze, the god's wind. I have been blowing God's wind from Heaven, so that several million people would change their mind through these two or three days.

3

Trump will end
The conflict in Middle East

And in addition to that, we, Happy Science, especially the members of the USA, acted politically. It might be the first experience for them. We are a religion born in Japan and usually counted as the minority-type of religion and, of course, our American members support the Democrats rather than the Republicans usually because they are requiring the equal rights for White-American, WASP people.

But this time, I predicted that now, it's time for strong president or it's time America should be America, America should be stronger. It's the last chance for them to make rebalance between the world powers because during the presidency of Mr. Barack Obama and these eight years, he has a tendency of withdrawing and declining. So, it's made the world more complicated.

For example, the trouble of the Syria and Iraq, I mean the IS. If there were not Mr. Obama and Mrs. Clinton, at that time, there would be no IS now. Mr. Obama's lure for peaceful world or Nobel Prize-like peaceful world caused the next turbulence in Iraq and Syria. There appeared ISIS and they are battling now. Donald Trump may cease the fire because he has such kind of ability and judgment and capability.

And Mr. Obama's great failure was his misunderstanding for Russia. He made the worst relationship between Russia and the United States. It's made quite opposite to his rebalance policy. It makes the world balance worse and worse. It makes Russia alone and lets Russia close to China.

Mr. Obama and Mrs. Clinton did nothing for the North Korean policy. They just pushed Beijing, I mean the People's Republic of China. But in reality, it means their weakness, I think so. If the president were Bush Jr., North Korea couldn't do such rude deeds again and again.

4

He is the president of 'Wisdom and courage'

So, Mr. Trump should learn a lot from today. But I think his intelligence is enough. He is the president of wisdom and courage. Wisdom and courage are most suitable for the forty-fifth president of the United States. They need wisdom.

Barack Obama is a clever person, but he doesn't have enough wisdom, I think so. Hillary also. But Mr. Trump has wisdom and he also has courage. TV reporters of Japan say that Beijing, I mean Xi Jinping, thinks that Hillary would be more difficult to deal with than Donald Trump, and Donald Trump is easy for them to deal with. But I think it's very contrary.

Hillary is the extension of Barack Obama's foreign policy, but Donald Trump would change their diplomatic policy because he is a thinkable man. And he will think of the foreign policy from scratch. He thinks of the world balance from the standpoint of equal-ness and fairness. That is my impression.

People of the world, especially Japanese foreign ministry or government, are just worrying about TPP or Trans-Pacific Partnership treaty. Of course, Donald Trump and Hillary Clinton both declared refusal to join the treaty, but we must think about this seriously, deeply.

5

Economic strategy against China

Donald Trump thinks that the tariff system, I mean the import tax system, is one of the weapons for diplomacy. He thinks so. It means, for example, he can use high tax rate for China if he doesn't like their foreign policy. For example, China wants to intrude some kind of Asian country. He will change the tax rate for China, the import tax rate for China. It is one of the weapons without hot war, without bullet, without missile, without the seventh fleet. He is just thinking this point.

I already said that the TPP is important for Japan because it was created as the counter power of the AIIB* of China. AIIB is the foreign policy which will make China the leader of the world, so we need the Trans-Pacific Partnership and no higher tax barrier regarding the Pacific Rim.

---

* Asia Infrastructure Investment Bank is a multilateral development bank for the Asian region. China took the initiative in establishing this institution in Dec. 2015, with 57 member states as its Founding Members.

It is Obama's thinking. Japan must join this policy. If not, China will win in foreign diplomacy and trading diplomacy with Africa and west part of Asia, and of course the north, south and east parts of Asia. And they can dispel the United States to Hawaii. This is their basic doctrine. So, we need TPP.

But Mr. Trump will rethink about this. Of course, Mr. Obama will persuade Donald Trump that he should join the TPP and the Japanese government is in a hurry to pass this alignment to the TPP. And before the retirement of Barack Obama, Japan will make a pressure to the United States to join this TPP before Mr. Trump takes office in the White House.

But now, at this point, we must think we have two ways. Of course, one is to join the TPP and guard the Transpacific trade and make prosperity, and another one is as Donald Trump said, "Make America greater again" and have new leadership for the world.

At this point, he said America is not the world's policeman, like Obama said, but it's not his real thinking, I think so. He will firstly rebuild the American economy and next, he will have hegemony in foreign affairs and in addition to that, he will want to remake the relationship between Russia and America.

Of course, he insisted that Japan should be Japan. He said so. I think this is truth and this is justice. Japan should be Japan. Japan is the world's second or third largest economic country. I said *the second* or *the third*; it means China's economic statistics is not believable. So, they have some kind of bubbly figures in their economic plan.

For example, they said that this year, the economic growth is 6.7 percent each quarter. It's a national growth planning rate; just the same rate. It's impossible in the real economy. The figure is very controlled for and they (Chinese communist officials) don't want to be fired by Xi Jinping, so we cannot rely on them. In reality, the real economy is not so different from, in conclusion, I mean Chinese and Japanese economic growth and power are not so different, I think so. It will be revealed in the near two or three years, I think so.

6

Two sides of Trump: Economic thinking and world justice

And Mr. Trump will insist that, as you know, Japanese mass media are upset by his saying that "Japan has a nuclear power" or "Japan is too big to protect. Japan should protect herself." He said so.

In reality, in the standpoint of logical thinking and realistic thinking and the pragmatic thinking and the economic thinking and the fair thinking, he is true. Japan is too big. World's second or third economy, and it cannot protect its own country? It's a mystery in the real meaning. So, he will say, "Protect yourself, or if Japan needs American protection or umbrella of nuclear weapon of the United States, Japan should pay more budget for defense cost of the U.S."

It will be choiceable for Japan. Of course, we can pay more or instead of that, we can protect by ourselves. It will give us a choice, but it does not mean Donald Trump is crazy or he's a tyrant. But he treated Japan as an equal partner and from the standpoint of equality and fairness, he said so. "Japan should protect herself. And South Korea, also, have enough power to protect itself from North Korea."

And especially, we must have keen attention on his opinion about the Spratly Islands issue. He said, "America should make more military force surge to the Spratly Islands." It indicates that he has the strategic idea or viewpoint he can rely on. He knows well.

Xi Jinping thinks that China is too big for America to have separation with, but it's not true. He has two kinds of thinking. One is the economic thinking, and another one is world justice. He's a businessman, so he can think about the real equal balance between China and America.

I think, in these 25 years, China has had huge economic growth, but Japan has been in status quo and America in trade deficit in these decades. It means America has been too weak in the economic trade meaning. So, he will change from the first point and this is good for creating world peace and world power balance, I think so.

7

America should play the role of World policeman again

And if I predict the next year and the following years of the United States and the world, I think we can sleep well, or we will sleep well from next year, because Japan and the United States reliance can be the world's main engine again, and the fundamental value of the U.S. and Japan will continue as the global criteria, so we can co-prosper for the next eight years. So, the result of the American presidential race was good for Japan and the world. We must check the world balance.

And of course, Mr. Barack Obama insisted on how to protect the human rights. It will be realized by the stronger America again, I think so. The world can have several hegemonic countries, but the main value for the human rights must be one. It is the meaning of democracy, freedom, and how to make world prosperity, and check the tyranny of the evil country. America should cooperate with another country and should play the role of the world policeman again, I think so.

This is my idea on the next day of the election of the United States presidency.

On Victory of Mr. Donald Trump

Q&A

Question 1

Guidance on how to unite The divided America after the election

Question 1

Guidance on how to unite the divided America after the election

Questioner
Kazuhiro Ichikawa
Senior Managing Director of Happy Science
Chief Director of International Headquarters

KAZUHIRO ICHIKAWA

Thank you very much, Master Okawa. Thank you for your deep insights and wisdom.

My question is on how to unite the people of America again because this election seems to have divided people into red or blue clearly. But in last night's Mr. Donald Trump's speech, he said, "It's time for us to come together as one united people." So, I would appreciate if you could give us guidance on how to create "united people."

RYUHO OKAWA

OK. As I told already, Mr. Trump is not a person who is comprehended by American mass media and Japanese mass media. He's quite a different person. He made too many extreme speeches, but in reality, he is a very moderate person and he has a very soft touch. He can keep very soft-touch relationship between people because he has lived to 70 years old and he has been a great businessman. So, he knows a lot about that. It's just been his strategy because he was not a politician. And he was not expected, so it was his strategy.

But as you heard yesterday, when he made a victory speech, firstly he said, "I received the call from Hillary Clinton, Mrs. Hillary Clinton, and she said, 'Congratulations.'" He appreciated her and he said she did a good job. This means he's quite different in reality. He knows, in real meaning, what it is, what she is, what he is, what man is, what men are, what the world is, what the economy is, and what politics is.

Hillary criticized him that he has no experience in politics and he has no experience of the army, and that he is the last man who can be believed to be a commander-in-chief, I mean the head of the American Army, the world number one army, and can use the nuclear code for nuclear missiles. Hillary criticized like that. But it's a misunderstanding on him. He can be a great politician and he is the most suitable person for commander-in-chief.

Commander-in-chief means he is the leader of the army and is required almighty capacity for everything. It's not only for war strategy, but also the commander-in-chief must know the world economy, world relationship and the morality, how to deal with another people of another country. But he knows in reality.

And he insisted the separation of the intruders from foreign countries. Now, at this time, it is essential for the United States to rethink about that, but it's not the eternal policy. I think so.

And in reality, American economy has been in great recession in these several years. They were replaced by foreign immigrants and they experienced a lot of dumping from Asian and African countries, so this is a very essential point for the rebirth of the United States in the economic meaning. He says he will build the [*laughs*] Trump wall between Mexico and the USA. It's interesting. He declared clearly, so will he try to build Trump wall or not? It's very exciting.

But he will use this condition for negotiation between Mexico and the United States, I think so. It's very important for the United States, how to stop the intruders from Mexico, especially people who have tendency to be criminals and tendency to be drug addicts. So, it's very important. It's the cancer within the United States. So, someone should check and stop this tendency.

I don't think he will make a new long wall of the Trump wall, but instead of that, he will save the intruder population from Mexico and check them if they are the criminal tendency or not, or drug-related people or not. It is very important for America.

But he, himself, is German-oriented person and his wife is from the east part of Europe, so he knows a lot about the one aspect of the immigrant that is good for America: to provide new, excellent people from the world, because America is a country of dream. So, every people or the people who want to succeed or want to come to the United States, some of them are very excellent and can be America's new engine for the future. He knows about that.

But before that, he must recheck about the immigrant policy, I think so. People of the world are astonished by his presidency, but I don't think so. In the next one year, he will think considerably and will make new strategy about that.

So, the dividing country's problem will change in the next real change of the United States. It's Obama's declaration eight years ago that he said he will change America. But the country's tendency is not good for the American future. So, Donald Trump will make real change for the rebirth of the great America or greater America. It's OK, we can accept.

America has many deficits, as you know, of course, the gun control problem, drug problem, or the difference between the rich and the poor. Of course, they have a lot of problems, but this is one of the greatest dream country of the world, so America should shine more and more. It will lead the world into the future, I guess so. So, the problem they say, "the divided America," will be conquered by Trump's real personality and realistic capability of his new governance power, I think so.

Question 2

Will Trump's lower tax policy

Be successful?

Question 2

Will Trump's lower tax policy be successful?

Questioner
Yuki Oikawa
Director of Foreign Affairs
Happiness Realization Party

YUKI OIKAWA

Master Okawa, thank you very much for today's lecture. Your lecture is very encouraging. Thank you very much.

Let me ask about the economic policy, especially tax policy. Mr. Obama's tax policy is higher tax, making a big government and redistributing the income to the minority people, especially poor people. Then, the U.S. had the worst economic recovery. So, it didn't succeed. And now, Mr. Trump said drastic lower tax such as 15 percent corporate tax. Now, the U.S. corporate tax is over 35 percent. People think this is ridiculous, so nobody believed that kind of policy and the mass media ignored his policy.

However, Master Okawa, you insisted the same kind of lower tax policy when you founded the Happiness Realization Party. So, what do you think about this kind of drastic lower tax policy to adopt in the U.S. and maybe in Japan?

RYUHO OKAWA

OK. It's a very important point. But Donald Trump will realize lower tax policy, I think so. It's essential for the rebirth of the United States. I said 15 percent is enough for private companies. When you earn 100, if you were taken 15 from government or another lower bureaucracy, it's enough, I think so. Thirty-five percent is too much. No work, but gain the profit only. It's a bad government, I think so. It's not an effective government, I think so.

Effective government means lower tax and make the private sector prosper more and more. It's the fundamental guideline for them. For example, even in Japan, the Abe government insisted that the Japanese corporations have inner money, about 370 trillion yen or so. He is targeting to get this inner-saving money from companies and to let them consume like Edo era's people, just consume and it will make prosperity of the economy, but this is a bad policy. In accordance with Japanese tradition, it's a bad *Tono-sama* [lord] president. We must save for the crisis, the future turbulence of the company's great decision, government's mistake, or foreign pressure. We must save money for the future. It is essential.

But there are greater-government policy people who can dream that a greater government or a big government will lead to an equal society. They are dreaming like that. That just means the idea of the communist declaration, I think so. Japan already has been caught by this kind of lure and if Mr. Trump changes the tax policy within the United States, Japan cannot insist the same policy. Japan must change their mind.

Government should work especially for non-profit area, I mean the realm. Profitable realm, it's for privatized, I mean the usual common companies area. And the nation's economy will receive more prosperity. Greater government, if in real meaning greater, it's OK, but if greater means just the gigantic government, it means it hires people who cannot work in the private realm, that kind of non-capable people, and pay their income from tax and lower the lost-job population.

Government usually wants to move to hire the jobless people and pay them from tax, so it means the company or people who worked hard and saved cost and produced profit will be taken more tax. And this tax will be used for the people who don't have a job now.

In some meaning, it's a good sense to create jobs, but in another sense, bureaucrats or bureaucracy means the incapable people or people who don't have enough power to earn money or make their living. It's the meaning of bureaucrats. So, the expansion of the members of bureaucracy is a bad news for the country, especially for future economy.

In Japan, we pay 1.5 times the income for public servants. It's bigger than the private sector. For example, if you get 400,000 yen for your winter bonus, a Japanese public servant can get 600,000 yen for his or her bonus. Why? Japanese government cannot answer this question, "Why?" If they pay more than private companies, it will mean the raise of the economy and the growth of the economy. Mr. Abe thinks like that. But it's bad, I mean, it's not the management-style thinking.

So, Donald Trump will change the story. Hillary criticized that the "trumped-up and trickle down," it means the economic pyramid, when the top of the economic pyramid becomes more wealthy, it will trickle down to the lower part of the people.

But it's false, Hillary said so. And democratic people, the poor people, are likely to think to get money forcibly from the upper class and give the helicopter money to the lower side of the people. In some meaning, it sounds like Christian thinking. Like Jesus said, if you are rich, give all things to others, but in reality, a businessman cannot do so. If he is management class, he cannot do so because he has responsibility to pay money and make the company a going concern company. It will need profit for him to keep his company and to hire his followers, so it's quite different.

America is not a country of Catholics, America is a Protestant country originally, so Protestants agree to get profit for prosperity and its prosperity will trickle down to every person of the nation. It is the Protestant thinking, I think so. So, if one is clever and wiser, he can get more money. It's reasonable. But if he has enough consciousness for God or poor people, he will use his income for good things. It depends on him, but he can do it.

It is one of the American traditions. It's more than Japanese tradition. Japanese tradition is less than American tradition. American people can do that, like Bill Gates or so. They can make great money, but they can use this money for the poor people of the world. It is America's most beautiful mind. I think so. Don't forget about the beautiful tradition.

So, America should not be a communist country. Japan also, deny to be a communist country. It means to just stop the gigantic government. It means a not effective government. The first step for that is to lower the tax rate and let the private companies do more for a better world. It is the main concept, I think so.

Question 3

How will America's relation With Russia change?

Question 3

How will America's relation with Russia change?

Questioner
Kazuhiro Takegawa
Director General of International Public Relations Division, Happy Science

KAZUHIRO TAKEGAWA
Thank you very much for today's speech, and much congratulations for yesterday.

May I ask a little more about diplomacy, especially the relationship with Russia? Master, you were talking about the Syrian War and how Mr. Trump would cease the fire. Also, Mr. Putin says the same thing. The Syrian War is called a proxy war. So, how can they deal with this war, for example? In this sense, Russia is fatal for America to be the world's policeman. Would you talk especially about the relation with Russia?

RYUHO OKAWA

OK. World question is how the relationship between Russia and America will change next year. My answer is, it will be for a good direction.

Mr. Putin and Mr. Trump can understand each other, as reported from the mass media. The mass media cannot understand the real meaning. Even Ms. Hillary Clinton cannot understand.

Usually, American people, especially the Republican people, think of Russia as an enemy. So, in the enemy country of Russia, the dictatorship of Putin has been continuing and Mr. Putin praised Mr. Trump, "He's a good man, and a reliable man." Donald Trump also said Putin has greater leadership than, as you know, Mr. Obama.

He's an honest person, I think so. This means "hero knows hero" as an old saying says so. *Eiyuu, eiyuu wo shiru*, "hero knows hero," that's the reason. So, Donald Trump and Mr. Putin also can esteem another person's power, capability, or virtue. They know each other and can respect each other.

So, the relationship between the two countries

will be better next year. And I predict, in the next year, I mean 2017, in one year, the problem of the IS will end because Russia and American relationship will determine the conclusion. Russia will have a power on Syria and America will regain the power on Iraq, and the IS will disappear in the end. That's the conclusion.

And during this process, we must make a good operation, how to reduce the killed people, I mean the non-army people, and how to save women and children. So, it will need American great will and Russian great will. The problem will end next year, I think so.

And the relationship between Putin and Trump will change the relationship between China and Japan, China and Russia, and China and North Korea. Mr. Xi Jinping thinks that Hillary will be stronger than Donald Trump, but in reality, it's quite contrary to that. Donald Trump will be stronger than Hillary because he knows the economy and foreign trade very deeply.

So, I can guess how he will deal with China.

He must think from the standpoint of the world economic equality or balance, and soon he will realize China's expansion rate is quite extraordinary. What's the problem? It's a problem of foreign currency exchange rate and the problem of the import tax rate.

He, Donald Trump, will call back the American corporations from China to the United States, and Japan will follow in some meaning. Japanese corporations will withdraw their companies from China to Japan and to inner production.

It's very essential. America changed its economic style from the first, second, third grades to the fourth grade, it means more than the service realm, for example, the financial planning level or like that. It means it's just the leverage for the economic field, not the real economy.

But Donald Trump realizes that the real economy is essential for the fundamentals of the country. He will regain the industry of the United States again. But he forgot that Japan doesn't have import taxes for American cars. American cars don't sell in Japan because they are too big to run on the Japanese roads. They are too big, too expensive, and too strong for Japan.

I once bought an American car, a Lincoln, for one year. It was about three tons and I could not turn right or left on the road enough because Japanese roads are very narrow. So, we could not control the car.

I bought that car because before that, there occurred the Aum affairs[*] in Japan, and Aum people wanted to shoot me. So, I bought a Lincoln and it, of course, had protection for bullets. But it was too heavy and I could not open the door by myself [*laughs*] [*audience laugh*].

But the positive point is, if I ride on the Lincoln, when we crash with a dump car, we can survive, even at that time. When we crash with a usual Japanese car, they will fly away, [*laughs*] so it's a positive point. But I sold it within a year because it's not so

---

[*] Aum Shinrikyo, a self-proclaimed new religion in Japan, committed an abduction and murder, and the subway sarin attack from Feb. to Mar. 1995. Happy Science had been criticizing Aum even before such events occurred and was cooperating with the police in investigating those cases. Later, the leader of Aum who was the mastermind behind the plan was given the death penalty.

easy for Japan to use that kind of heavy, deluxe car. And, how do I say, everyone could know who I am and what this car was, so it was not so good. So, I changed it to a Toyota car [*audience laugh*]. This is the reason. Donald Trump never thinks about that, but he will know soon.

ABOUT THE AUTHOR

Founder and CEO of Happy Science Group.

Ryuho Okawa was born on July 7th 1956, in Tokushima, Japan. After graduating from the University of Tokyo with a law degree, he joined a Tokyo-based trading house. While working at its New York headquarters, he studied international finance at the Graduate Center of the City University of New York. In 1981, he attained Great Enlightenment and became aware that he is El Cantare with a mission to bring salvation to all humankind.

In 1986, he established Happy Science. It now has members in over 166 countries across the world, with more than 700 branches and temples as well as 10,000 missionary houses around the world.

He has given over 3,450 lectures (of which more than 150 are in English) and published over 3,100 books (of which more than 600 are Spiritual Interview Series), and many are translated into 41 languages. Along with *The Laws of the Sun* and *The Laws of Hell*, many of the books have become best sellers or million sellers. To date, Happy Science has produced 26 movies. The original story and original concept were given by the Executive Producer Ryuho Okawa. He has also composed music and written lyrics of over 450 pieces.

Moreover, he is the Founder of Happy Science University and Happy Science Academy (Junior and Senior High School), Founder and President of the Happiness Realization Party, Founder and Honorary Headmaster of Happy Science Institute of Government and Management, Founder of IRH Press Co., Ltd., and the Chairperson of NEW STAR PRODUCTION Co., Ltd. and ARI Production Co., Ltd.

WHAT IS EL CANTARE?

El Cantare means "the Light of the Earth," and is the Supreme God of the Earth who has been guiding humankind since the beginning of Genesis. He is whom Jesus called Father and Muhammad called Allah, and is *Ame-no-Mioya-Gami*, Japanese Father God. Different parts of El Cantare's core consciousness have descended to Earth in the past, once as Alpha and another as Elohim. His branch spirits, such as Shakyamuni Buddha and Hermes, have descended to Earth many times and helped to flourish many civilizations. To unite various religions and to integrate various fields of study in order to build a new civilization on Earth, a part of the core consciousness has descended to Earth as Master Ryuho Okawa.

Alpha is a part of the core consciousness of El Cantare who descended to Earth around 330 million years ago. Alpha preached Earth's Truths to harmonize and unify Earth-born humans and space people who came from other planets.

Elohim is a part of El Cantare's core consciousness who descended to Earth around 150 million years ago. He gave wisdom, mainly on the differences of light and darkness, good and evil.

Ame-no-Mioya-Gami (Japanese Father God) is the Creator God and the Father God who appears in the ancient literature, *Hotsuma Tsutae*. It is believed that He descended on the foothills of Mt. Fuji about 30,000 years ago and built the Fuji dynasty, which is the root of the Japanese civilization. With justice as the central pillar, Ame-no-Mioya-Gami's teachings spread to ancient civilizations of other countries in the world.

Shakyamuni Buddha was born as a prince into the Shakya Clan in India around 2,600 years ago. When he was 29 years old, he renounced the world and sought enlightenment. He later attained Great Enlightenment and founded Buddhism.

Hermes is one of the 12 Olympian gods in Greek mythology, but the spiritual Truth is that he taught the teachings of love and progress around 4,300 years ago that became the origin of the current Western civilization. He is a hero that truly existed.

Ophealis was born in Greece around 6,500 years ago and was the leader who took an expedition to as far as Egypt. He is the God of miracles, prosperity, and arts, and is known as Osiris in the Egyptian mythology.

Rient Arl Croud was born as a king of the ancient Incan Empire around 7,000 years ago and taught about the mysteries of the mind. In the heavenly world, he is responsible for the interactions that take place between various planets.

Thoth was an almighty leader who built the golden age of the Atlantic civilization around 12,000 years ago. In the Egyptian mythology, he is known as god Thoth.

Ra Mu was a leader who built the golden age of the civilization of Mu around 17,000 years ago. As a religious leader and a politician, he ruled by uniting religion and politics.

WHAT IS A SPIRITUAL MESSAGE?

We are all spiritual beings living on this earth. The following is the mechanism behind Master Ryuho Okawa's spiritual messages.

1 You are a spirit

People are born into this world to gain wisdom through various experiences and return to the other world when their lives end. We are all spirits and repeat this cycle in order to refine our souls.

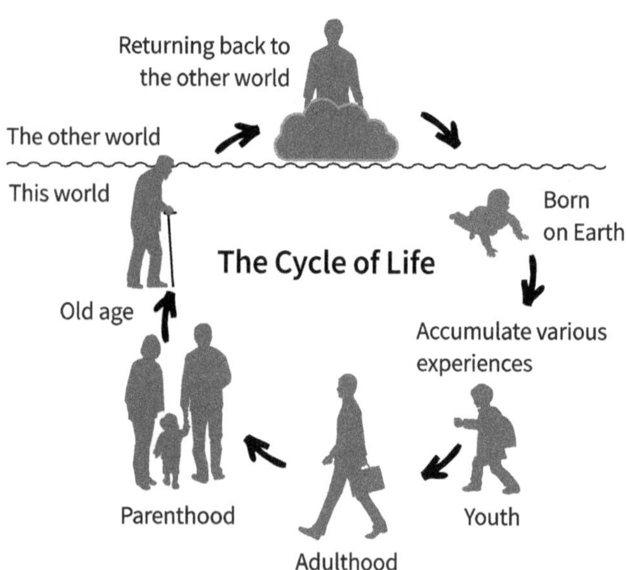

2 You have a guardian spirit

Guardian spirits are those who protect the people who are living on this earth. Each of us has a guardian spirit that watches over us and guides us from the other world. They were us in our past life, and are identical in how we think.

3 How spiritual messages work

Master Ryuho Okawa, through his enlightenment, is capable of summoning any spirit from anywhere in the world, including the spirit world.

Master Okawa's way of receiving spiritual messages is fundamentally different from that of other psychic mediums who undergo trances and are thereby completely taken over by the spirits they are channeling.

Master Okawa's attainment of a high level of enlightenment enables him to retain full control of his consciousness and body throughout the duration of the spiritual message. To allow the spirits to express their own thoughts and personalities freely, however, Master Okawa usually softens the dominancy of his consciousness. This way, he is able to keep his own philosophies out of the way and ensure that the spiritual messages are pure expressions of the spirits he is channeling.

Since guardian spirits think at the same subconscious level as the person living on earth, Master Okawa can summon the spirit and find out what the person on earth is actually thinking. If the person has already returned to the other world, the spirit can give messages to the people living on earth through Master Okawa.

Since 2009, many spiritual messages have been openly recorded by Master Okawa and published. Spiritual messages from the guardian spirits of people living today such as Donald Trump, former Japanese Prime Minister Shinzo Abe and Chinese President Xi Jinping, as well as spiritual messages sent from the spirit world by Jesus Christ, Muhammad, Thomas Edison, Mother Teresa, Steve Jobs and Nelson Mandela are just a tiny pack of spiritual messages that were published so far.

Domestically, in Japan, these spiritual messages are being read by a wide range of politicians and mass media, and the high-level contents of these books are delivering an impact even more on politics, news and public opinion. In recent years, there have been spiritual messages recorded in English, and

English translations are being done on the spiritual messages given in Japanese. These have been published overseas, one after another, and have started to shake the world.

For more about spiritual messages and a complete list of books in the Spiritual Interview Series, visit okawabooks.com

ABOUT HAPPY SCIENCE

Happy Science is a global movement that empowers individuals to find purpose and spiritual happiness and to share that happiness with their families, societies, and the world. With more than 12 million members around the world, Happy Science aims to increase awareness of spiritual truths and expand our capacity for love, compassion, and joy so that together we can create the kind of world we all wish to live in.

Activities at Happy Science are based on the Principle of Happiness (Love, Wisdom, Self-Reflection, and Progress). This principle embraces worldwide philosophies and beliefs, transcending boundaries of culture and religions.

Love teaches us to give ourselves freely without expecting anything in return; it encompasses giving, nurturing, and forgiving.

Wisdom leads us to the insights of spiritual truths, and opens us to the true meaning of life and the will of God (the universe, the highest power, Buddha).

Self-Reflection brings a mindful, nonjudgmental lens to our thoughts and actions to help us find our truest selves—the essence of our souls—and deepen our connection to the highest power. It helps us attain a clean and peaceful mind and leads us to the right life path.

Progress emphasizes the positive, dynamic aspects of our spiritual growth—actions we can take to manifest and spread happiness around the world. It's a path that not only expands our soul growth, but also furthers the collective potential of the world we live in.

PROGRAMS AND EVENTS

The doors of Happy Science are open to all. We offer a variety of programs and events, including self-exploration and self-growth programs, spiritual seminars, meditation and contemplation sessions, study groups, and book events.

Our programs are designed to:

* Deepen your understanding of your purpose and meaning in life
* Improve your relationships and increase your capacity to love unconditionally
* Attain peace of mind, decrease anxiety and stress, and feel positive
* Gain deeper insights and a broader perspective on the world
* Learn how to overcome life's challenges

... and much more.

For more information, visit happy-science.org.

OUR ACTIVITIES

Happy Science does other various activities to provide support for those in need.

- **You Are An Angel! General Incorporated Association**

  Happy Science has a volunteer network in Japan that encourages and supports children with disabilities as well as their parents and guardians.

- **Never Mind School for Truancy**

  At 'Never Mind,' we support students who find it very challenging to attend schools in Japan. We also nurture their self-help spirit and power to rebound against obstacles in life based on Master Okawa's teachings and faith.

- **"Prevention Against Suicide" Campaign since 2003**

  A nationwide campaign to reduce suicides; over 20,000 people commit suicide every year in Japan. "The Suicide Prevention Website-Words of Truth for You-" presents spiritual prescriptions for worries such as depression, lost love, extramarital affairs, bullying and work-related problems, thereby saving many lives.

- **Support for Anti-bullying Campaigns**

  Happy Science provides support for a group of parents and guardians, Network to Protect Children from Bullying, a general incorporated foundation launched in Japan to end bullying, including those that can even be called a criminal offense. So far, the network received more than 5,000 cases and resolved 90% of them.

- **The Golden Age Scholarship**

  This scholarship is granted to students who can contribute greatly and bring a hopeful future to the world.

- **Success No.1**
  Buddha's Truth Afterschool Academy

  Happy Science has over 180 classrooms throughout Japan and in several cities around the world that focus on afterschool education for children. The education focuses on faith and morals in addition to supporting children's school studies.

- **Angel Plan V**

  For children under the age of kindergarten, Happy Science holds classes for nurturing healthy, positive, and creative boys and girls.

- **Future Stars Training Department**

  The Future Stars Training Department was founded within the Happy Science Media Division with the goal of nurturing talented individuals to become successful in the performing arts and entertainment industry.

- **NEW STAR PRODUCTION Co., Ltd.**
  ARI Production Co., Ltd.

  We have companies to nurture actors and actresses, artists, and vocalists. They are also involved in film production.

CONTACT INFORMATION

Happy Science is a worldwide organization with branches and temples around the globe. For a comprehensive list, visit the worldwide directory at *happy-science.org*. The following are some of the many Happy Science locations:

United States and Canada

New York
79 Franklin St., New York, NY 10013, USA
Phone: 1-212-343-7972
Fax: 1-212-343-7973
Email: ny@happy-science.org
Website: happyscience-usa.org

New Jersey
66 Hudson St., #2R, Hoboken, NJ 07030, USA
Phone: 1-201-313-0127
Email: nj@happy-science.org
Website: happyscience-usa.org

Chicago
2300 Barrington Rd., Suite #400,
Hoffman Estates, IL 60169, USA
Phone: 1-630-937-3077
Email: chicago@happy-science.org
Website: happyscience-usa.org

Florida
5208 8th St., Zephyrhills, FL 33542, USA
Phone: 1-813-715-0000
Fax: 1-813-715-0010
Email: florida@happy-science.org
Website: happyscience-usa.org

Atlanta
1874 Piedmont Ave., NE Suite 360-C
Atlanta, GA 30324, USA
Phone: 1-404-892-7770
Email: atlanta@happy-science.org
Website: happyscience-usa.org

San Francisco
525 Clinton St.
Redwood City, CA 94062, USA
Phone & Fax: 1-650-363-2777
Email: sf@happy-science.org
Website: happyscience-usa.org

Los Angeles
1590 E. Del Mar Blvd., Pasadena, CA
91106, USA
Phone: 1-626-395-7775
Fax: 1-626-395-7776
Email: la@happy-science.org
Website: happyscience-usa.org

Orange County
16541 Gothard St. Suite 104
Huntington Beach, CA 92647
Phone: 1-714-659-1501
Email: oc@happy-science.org
Website: happyscience-usa.org

San Diego
7841 Balboa Ave. Suite #202
San Diego, CA 92111, USA
Phone: 1-626-395-7775
Fax: 1-626-395-7776
E-mail: sandiego@happy-science.org
Website: happyscience-usa.org

Hawaii
Phone: 1-808-591-9772
Fax: 1-808-591-9776
Email: hi@happy-science.org
Website: happyscience-usa.org

Kauai
3343 Kanakolu Street, Suite 5
Lihue, HI 96766, USA
Phone: 1-808-822-7007
Fax: 1-808-822-6007
Email: kauai-hi@happy-science.org
Website: happyscience-usa.org

Toronto
845 The Queensway
Etobicoke, ON M8Z 1N6, Canada
Phone: 1-416-901-3747
Email: toronto@happy-science.org
Website: happy-science.ca

Vancouver
#201-2607 East 49th Avenue,
Vancouver, BC, V5S 1J9, Canada
Phone: 1-604-437-7735
Fax: 1-604-437-7764
Email: vancouver@happy-science.org
Website: happy-science.ca

INTERNATIONAL

Tokyo
1-6-7 Togoshi, Shinagawa,
Tokyo, 142-0041, Japan
Phone: 81-3-6384-5770
Fax: 81-3-6384-5776
Email: tokyo@happy-science.org
Website: happy-science.org

Seoul
74, Sadang-ro 27-gil,
Dongjak-gu, Seoul, Korea
Phone: 82-2-3478-8777
Fax: 82-2-3478-9777
Email: korea@happy-science.org
Website: happyscience-korea.org

London
3 Margaret St.
London, W1W 8RE United Kingdom
Phone: 44-20-7323-9255
Fax: 44-20-7323-9344
Email: eu@happy-science.org
Website: www.happyscience-uk.org

Taipei
No. 89, Lane 155, Dunhua N. Road,
Songshan District, Taipei City 105, Taiwan
Phone: 886-2-2719-9377
Fax: 886-2-2719-5570
Email: taiwan@happy-science.org
Website: happyscience-tw.org

Sydney
516 Pacific Highway, Lane Cove North,
2066 NSW, Australia
Phone: 61-2-9411-2877
Fax: 61-2-9411-2822
Email: sydney@happy-science.org

Kuala Lumpur
No 22A, Block 2, Jalil Link Jalan Jalil
Jaya 2, Bukit Jalil 57000,
Kuala Lumpur, Malaysia
Phone: 60-3-8998-7877
Fax: 60-3-8998-7977
Email: malaysia@happy-science.org
Website: happyscience.org.my

Sao Paulo
Rua. Domingos de Morais 1154,
Vila Mariana, Sao Paulo SP
CEP 04010-100, Brazil
Phone: 55-11-5088-3800
Email: sp@happy-science.org
Website: happyscience.com.br

Kathmandu
Kathmandu Metropolitan City,
Ward No. 15, Ring Road, Kimdol,
Sitapaila Kathmandu, Nepal
Phone: 977-1-427-2931
Email: nepal@happy-science.org

Jundiai
Rua Congo, 447, Jd. Bonfiglioli
Jundiai-CEP, 13207-340, Brazil
Phone: 55-11-4587-5952
Email: jundiai@happy-science.org

Kampala
Plot 877 Rubaga Road, Kampala
P.O. Box 34130 Kampala, UGANDA
Email: uganda@happy-science.org

ABOUT HAPPINESS REALIZATION PARTY

The Happiness Realization Party (HRP) was founded in May 2009 by Master Ryuho Okawa as part of the Happy Science Group. HRP strives to improve the Japanese society, based on three basic political principles of "freedom, democracy, and faith," and let Japan promote individual and public happiness from Asia to the world as a leader nation.

1) Diplomacy and Security: Protecting Freedom, Democracy, and Faith of Japan and the World from China's Totalitarianism

Japan's current defense system is insufficient against China's expanding hegemony and the threat of North Korea's nuclear missiles. Japan, as the leader of Asia, must strengthen its defense power and promote strategic diplomacy together with the nations which share the values of freedom, democracy, and faith. Further, HRP aims to realize world peace under the leadership of Japan, the nation with the spirit of religious tolerance.

2) Economy: Early economic recovery through utilizing the "wisdom of the private sector"

Economy has been damaged severely by the novel coronavirus originated in China. Many companies have been forced into bankruptcy or out of business. What is needed for economic recovery now is not subsidies and regulations by the government, but policies which can utilize the "wisdom of the private sector."

For more information, visit en.hr-party.jp

HAPPY SCIENCE ACADEMY JUNIOR AND SENIOR HIGH SCHOOL

Happy Science Academy Junior and Senior High School is a boarding school founded with the goal of educating the future leaders of the world who can have a big vision, persevere, and take on new challenges.

Currently, there are two campuses in Japan; the Nasu Main Campus in Tochigi Prefecture, founded in 2010, and the Kansai Campus in Shiga Prefecture, founded in 2013.

HAPPY SCIENCE UNIVERSITY

THE FOUNDING SPIRIT AND THE GOAL OF EDUCATION

Based on the founding philosophy of the university, "Exploration of happiness and the creation of a new civilization," education, research and studies will be provided to help students acquire deep understanding grounded in religious belief and advanced expertise with the objectives of producing "great talents of virtue" who can contribute in a broad-ranging way to serve Japan and the international society.

FACULTIES

Faculty of human happiness

Students in this faculty will pursue liberal arts from various perspectives with a multidisciplinary approach, explore and envision an ideal state of human beings and society.

Faculty of successful management

This faculty aims to realize successful management that helps organizations to create value and wealth for society and to contribute to the happiness and the development of management and employees as well as society as a whole.

Faculty of future creation

Students in this faculty study subjects such as political science, journalism, performing arts and artistic expression, and explore and present new political and cultural models based on truth, goodness and beauty.

Faculty of future industry

This faculty aims to nurture engineers who can resolve various issues facing modern civilization from a technological standpoint and contribute to the creation of new industries of the future.

ABOUT HS PRESS

HS Press is an imprint of IRH Press Co., Ltd. IRH Press Co., Ltd., based in Tokyo, was founded in 1987 as a publishing division of Happy Science. IRH Press publishes religious and spiritual books, journals, magazines and also operates broadcast and film production enterprises. For more information, visit *okawabooks.com*.

Follow us on:

- Facebook: Okawa Books
- Instagram: OkawaBooks
- Youtube: Okawa Books
- Twitter: Okawa Books
- Pinterest: Okawa Books
- Goodreads: Ryuho Okawa

NEWSLETTER

To receive book related news, promotions and events, please subscribe to our newsletter below.

eepurl.com/bsMeJj

AUDIO / VISUAL MEDIA

YOUTUBE

PODCAST

Introduction of Ryuho Okawa's titles; topics ranging from self-help, current affairs, spirituality, religion, and the universe.

BOOKS BY RYUHO OKAWA

RYUHO OKAWA'S LAWS SERIES

The Laws Series is an annual volume of books that are comprised of Ryuho Okawa's lectures that function as universal guidance to all people. They are of various topics that were given in accordance with the changes that each year brings. *The Laws of the Sun*, the first publication of the laws series, ranked in the annual best-selling list in Japan in 1994. Since, the laws series' titles have ranked in the annual best-selling list every year for more than two decades, setting socio-cultural trends in Japan and around the world.

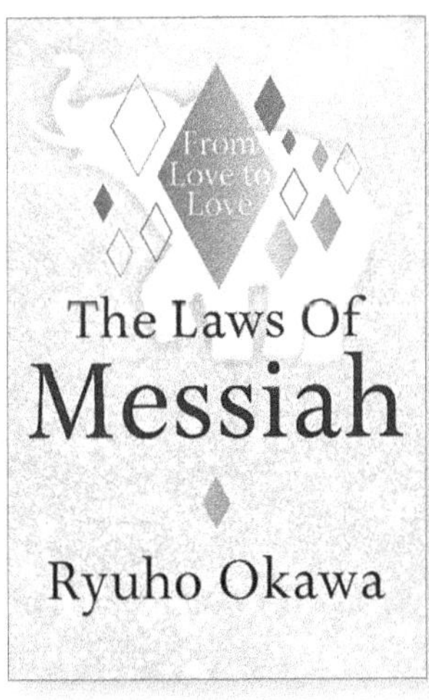

The 28th Laws Series

The Laws Of Messiah

From Love to Love

Paperback • 248 pages • $16.95
ISBN: 978-1-942125-90-7 (Jan. 31, 2022)

"What is Messiah?" This book carries an important message of love and guidance to people living now from the Modern-Day Messiah or the Modern-Day Savior. It also reveals the secret of Shambhala, the spiritual center of Earth, as well as the truth that this spiritual center is currently in danger of perishing and what we can do to protect this sacred place.

Love your Lord God. Know that those who don't know love don't know God. Discover the true love of God and the ideal practice of faith. This book teaches the most important element we must not lose sight of as we go through our soul training on this planet Earth.

SPIRITUAL INTERVIEW WITH GEORGE WASHINGTON

REVEALING DONALD TRUMP'S HIDDEN IDENTITY

What would George Washington say about today's America? Read this and find out! America's Founding Father's current thoughts on Racial problems, America's foreign policies, The American and world economies, and his mission and the secret of his soul.

1 America's Founding Father Washington Appears

2 In the American Presidential Election, he Supports the"Honest Man"

3 On Racial Problems in Current America

4 He Helped God Make a New Civilization

5 On America's Foreign Policies on the Middle East and Russia

6 On American and World Economies

7 On Problems with North Korea

8 The Secret of the God of America

9 His Past Lives as a God in India, Europe, and Africa

10 Declaring His Rebirth as Donald Trump

THE TRUMP SECRET

SEEING THROUGH THE PAST, PRESENT, AND FUTURE OF THE NEW AMERICAN PRESIDENT

Donald Trump's victory in the 2016 presidential election surprised almost all major vote forecasters who predicted Hillary Clinton's victory. But 10 months earlier, in January 2016, Ryuho Okawa, Global Visionary, a renowned spiritual leader, and international best-selling author, had already foreseen Trump's victory. This book contains a series of lectures and interviews that unveil the secrets to Trump's victory and makes predictions of what will happen under his presidency. This book predicts the coming of a new America that will go through a great transformation from the "red and blue states" to the United States.

CONTENTS

Samurai President of the Philippines

Spiritual Interview with the Guardian Spirit of Rodrigo Duterte

Samurai President of the Philippines contains the spiritual interview with the subconscious of President Duterte, and reveals that the president is the reincarnation of the internationally renowned, proud Japanese military officer. The secret to his hard-lined leadership of executing over one thousand drug offenders lies in his past life as a Japanese general who fought a deadly battle. Here is the nature of his soul and the true mind of the "samurai president" who will be a key person in Asia from now on.

1 Looking through the Mind of the Mysterious President Duterte
2 Impression of the Visit to Japan and of Prime Minister Abe
3 "Just Kill Bad People"
4 How Does He See America and Japan as the God of the Philippines?
5 The Guardian Spirit Reveals His True Thinking on China
6 His Outlook on the South China Sea Problem with China
7 The Guardian Spirit's Vision of the Asian Century
8 Revealing His Deep Connection to Japan and Speaking in Japanese
9 Regain the Spirit of Meiji and Stand Up, Japan
10 Underground Plans for a New Worldview
11 After the Spiritual Interview from the Guardian Spirit of Duterte

PUTIN'S INSIGHTS ON RUSSIA, JAPAN AND THE WORLD

AN INTERVIEW WITH THE GUARDIAN SPIRIT OF THE PRESIDENT OF RUSSIA

In this book, Master Okawa summons the guardian spirit of President Putin and asks his opinion on the current world leaders, how he looks upon Syrian affairs and the confusion in the EU, and on what he predicts will happen in the next 5 years with the Asian crisis.

1 President Putin's Guardian Spirit Appeared the Day After Abe-Putin Talks
2 "Abe's Basic Strategy is Wrong"
3 Can Japan Afford to Lose Its Friendship with Russia?
4 What is Lacking in Japanese Politics?
5 World Leaders in the Eyes of Putin's Guardian Spirit
6 Both Russia and China Could Become Potential Enemies of Japan
7 On Syrian Affairs and EU Confusion
8 Asian Crisis within the Next 5 years
9 How Can Japan Become Truly Independent?
10 What Putin's Guardian Spirit Expects of Happy Science
11 The "Excellent Move" Needed in the Japan-Russia Affairs
12 After the Third Spiritual Interview with Putin's Guardian Spirit

A New Message From Barack Obama

Interviewing the Guardian Spirit of the President of the United States

This spiritual interview reveals President Obama's stance on international relations. Now that America is "on the verge of crisis," as the guardian spirit of President Obama says in this interview, we all need to think about how we can achieve security, justice and peace in the world without the "world's policeman."

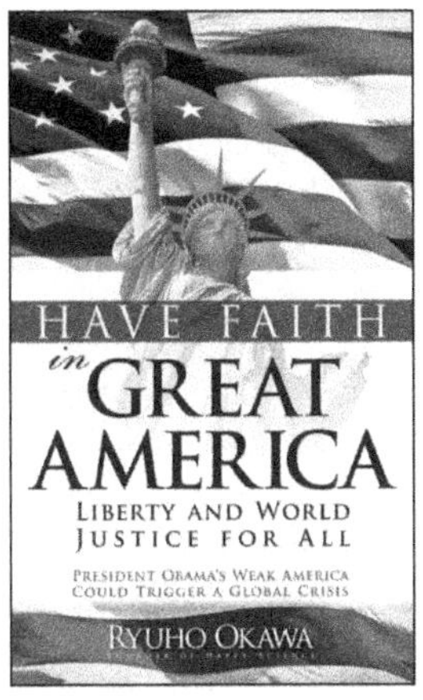

HAVE FAITH IN GREAT AMERICA

LIBERTY AND WORLD JUSTICE FOR ALL: PRESIDENT OBAMA'S WEAK AMERICA COULD TRIGGER A GLOBAL CRISIS

Have Faith in Great America: Liberty and World Justice for All is Master Ryuho Okawa's earnest message to the United States of America. The world's future depends on America's fulfillment of its long-held sacred mission of protecting the faith, liberty, and justice of people and nations around the world, and on the development of strong bonds between the United States and Japan. Today, the course of world history has reached a critical turning point. We all saw 2012's most pivotal events come to pass in November: the reelection of United States President Barack Obama, as well as Xi Jinping's selection as the next president of China, which marks the beginning of an entire decade under his authority.

Chapter One - The American Mind

Chapter Two - Why We Can't Wait

Chapter Three - Solutions to America's Crisis Why We Can't Wait: Q&A

Chapter Four - Spiritual Interview with Reelected President Obama

Chapter Five - An Interview with the Guardian Spirit of Barack Obama

INTO THE STORM OF INTERNATIONAL POLITICS

THE NEW STANDARDS OF THE WORLD ORDER

The world is now seeking a new idea or a new philosophy that will show the countries with such values the direction they should head in. In this book, Okawa presents new standards of the world order while giving his own analysis on world affairs concerning the U.S., China, Islamic State and others.

RYUHO OKAWA - A POLITICAL REVOLUTIONARY

THE ORIGINATOR OF ABENOMICS AND FATHER OF THE HAPPINESS REALIZATION PARTY

In this book, the Founder and the Master of Happy Science Group as well as the Father of Happiness Realization Party, Master Okawa lays down the guiding principles and the ways to breakthrough on the topics of economy, finance, nuclear power plant, foreign diplomacy, social welfare, and society with aging population and a falling birth rate.

THE MANIFESTO OF THE HAPPINESS REALIZATION PARTY

This book is a historical declaration to change the world through a peaceful revolution by the philosophy and speech based on the Truth, rather than by violence or massacre. It also states on the assessment of the meaning of WWII as well as how the relation between religion and politics should be. It is a must read for all people who wish to build a true utopia.

THE POWER TO LEAD THE WORLD

"It is not enough to speak only of ideals; we must envision how this world should be while setting our eyes firmly on things like real politics."

–Master Ryuho Okawa

[This book is available only in local branches and temples. Please refer to the contact information.]

For a complete list of books, visit okawabooks.com

The Laws of the Sun

ONE SOURCE, ONE PLANET, ONE PEOPLE

Imagine if you could ask God why He created this world and what spiritual laws He used to shape us—and everything around us. If we could understand His designs and intentions, we could discover what our goals in life should be and whether our actions move us closer to those goals or farther away.

The Golden Laws

HISTORY THROUGH THE EYES OF THE ETERNAL BUDDHA

The Golden Laws reveals how Buddha's Plan has been unfolding on earth, and outlines five thousand years of the secret history of humankind. Once we understand the true course of history, we cannot help but become aware of the significance of our spiritual mission in the present age.

The Nine Dimensions

UNVEILING THE LAWS OF ETERNITY

This book is a window into the mind of our loving God, who encourages us to grow into greater angels. It reveals His deepest intentions, answering the timely question of why He conceived such a colorful medley of religions, philosophies, sciences, arts, and other forms of expression.

For a complete list of books, visit okawabooks.com

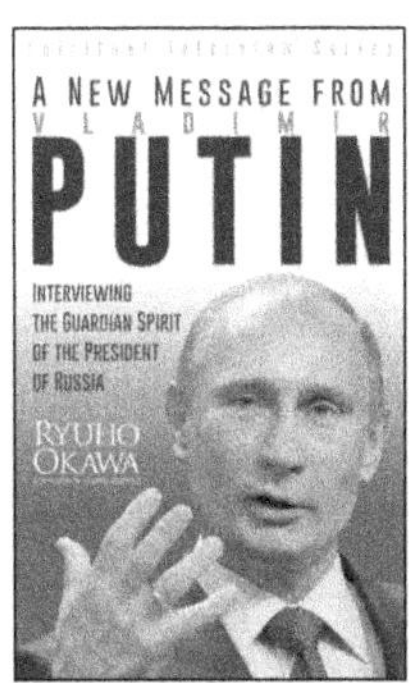

A NEW MESSAGE FROM VLADIMIR PUTIN

INVERVIEWING THE GUARDIAN SPIRIT OF THE PRESIDENT OF RUSSIA

We hereby bring you the spiritual message from the guardian spirit of President Putin, the politician who is the center of attention of not just the people of Russia but of the whole world, regardless of it being in a good or a bad way. In the Preface, it says, "President Putin's true intentions, which are 90 percent misunderstood."

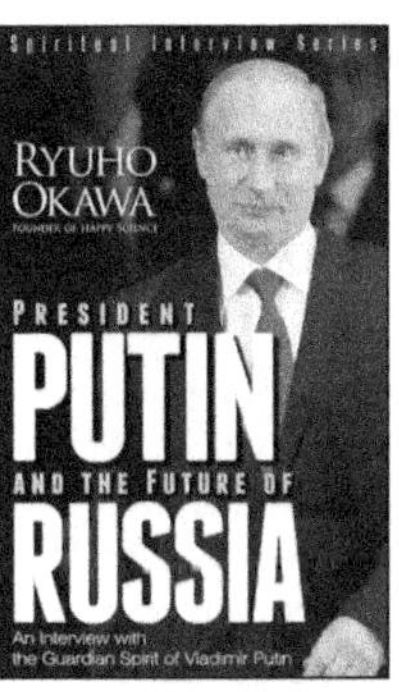

PRESIDENT PUTIN AND THE FUTURE OF RUSSIA

AN INTERVIEW WITH THE GUARDIAN SPIRIT OF VLADIMIR PUTIN

"I have no intention of fighting the United States. The Cold War is over... I have no intention of fighting the Americans... And I'm not friendly enough with China to think about joining them against the United States... I have given Russians religious freedom, which makes me very different from the Chinese."

–Putin's Guardian Spirit

CHINA'S HIDDEN AGENDA

THE MASTERMIND BEHIND THE ANTI-AMERICAN AND ANTI-JAPANESE PROTESTS

"I wanted to stir up the anti-American movement in the Arab world to make sure that the United States won't be able to attack Syria or Iran...I'm the mastermind behind the Muhammad video."

–Xi Jinping's Guardian Spirit

For a complete list of books, visit okawabooks.com

INTERVIEWING THE GUARDIAN SPIRIT OF U.S AMBASSADOR CAROLINE KENNEDY

A NEW BRIDGE BETWEEN JAPAN AND THE U.S.

What is Ambassador Kennedy's views on Japan-U. S. and Japan-China relations? How does she view World War II? What was the reason behind the Kennedy tragedies? What does she seek from the Japanese and American people? Find the answers in this book.

WAS DROPPING THE ATOMIC BOMBS A CRIME AGAINST HUMANITY?

INSIGHTS FROM HARRY S. TRUMAN
AND FRANKLIN D. ROOSEVELT

Was there any true justification for the atomic bombing? To answer to this question, Master Ryuho Okawa conducted spiritual interviews with Truman and Roosevelt. This book reveals valuable information that will help the world gain a truthful understanding of world history.

THE TRUTH OF THE PACIFIC WAR

SOULFUL MESSAGES FROM HIDEKI TOJO,
JAPAN'S WARTIME LEADER
INCLUDING A SPIRITUAL INTERVIEW WITH
GENERAL DOUGLAS MACARTHUR

The material provided is a testimony by General Hideki Tojo, who was Japan's most significant figure in the Pacific War. Furthermore, we have also recorded a testimony by Supreme Commander of the Allied Powers Douglas MacArthur in order to ensure a fair argument.

For a complete list of books, visit okawabooks.com

CRITIQUE OF CURRENT WORLD AFFAIRS

IMMANUEL KANT'S ADVICE FROM HEAVEN

"We can clearly see from Kant's message that we constantly need to enlighten people in order to prevent humankind from falling into a dangerous, hellish way of thinking."

—From Preface

[This book is available only in local branches and temples. Please refer to the contact information.]

MARGARET THATCHER'S MIRACULOUS MESSAGE

AN INTERVIEW WITH THE IRON LADY 19 HOURS AFTER HER DEATH

On April 9, 2013, just nineteen hours after Margaret Thatcher's death, Master Ryuho Okawa summoned her spirit to hold a spiritual interview. Her words will prove helpful not only to the United Kingdom, but also to the global economy and governments all over the world, including those of the United States and the European Union.

THE NEW DIPLOMATIC STRATEGIES OF SIR WINSTON CHURCHILL

A SPIRITUAL INTERVIEW WITH THE FORMER PRIME MINISTER REGARDING THE AGE OF PERSEVERANCE

If there is a chance to hear the opinion of Sir Winston Churchill on current international affairs, journalists around the world will probably be interested to hear this. This book made this possible.

For a complete list of books, visit okawabooks.com

Nelson Mandela's Last Message

A Conversation with Madiba Six Hours After His Death

As Mandela's spirit says in this spiritual interview, God created our souls as thinking energy without color, and that our colorless soul is the basis of our fundamental freedom and equality. In this spiritual interview, Master Ryuho Okawa gives us a glimpse into the mind of this great leader whose undefeated spirit is a message of hope to us all.

Mother Teresa's Current Calling in Heaven

The Saint of the Gutters Delivers Her Experiences of God, Heaven, and Our Mission

In this spiritual interview, Mother Teresa's spirit talks about her astonishing discoveries about God, Heaven, and the mission that people on earth should aim to fulfill through life. She reveals that the other world is a vast place with many levels of angels, that Heaven and Hell exist, and that the reality of the human being is the soul.

On Happiness Revolution

A Spiritual Interview with Hannah Arendt

In this book, the German-born Jewish American political theorist offers a spiritual lecture on democracy, on totalitarianism in East Asia, on communism and equality, on the Love of God and Justice of God, as well as her mission as a prophet of the new age.

For a complete list of books, visit okawabooks.com

ARE ISLAMIC EXTREMISTS JIHADISTS OR TERRORISTS?

THE NECESSITY OF FREEDOM IN ISLAMIC COUNTRIES

"As the world teacher, it was my duty to determine from a religious perspective whether it is true that the militant Islamic extremists are terrorist organizations, as the West calls them, or whether we should accept them as jihadists of pure faith. I found the answer in this interview."

-From Afterword

THE JUST CAUSE IN THE IRAQ WAR

DID SADDAM HUSSEIN POSSESS WEAPONS OF MASS DESTRUCTION?

In this book, you will discover that Saddam Hussein was also behind the planning of the 9/11 terrorist attacks and both he and Osama bin Laden are now in Hell. The knowledge this book provides will help each of us make the right decisions as we work together to create a peaceful international society.

A SPIRITUAL INTERVIEW WITH THE LEADER OF ISIL, AL-BAGHDADI

INCLUDING SPIRITUAL INVESTIGATION INTO THE TRUTH OF THE JAPANESE HOSTAGE TAKING

The author believes we must see through the destiny of ISIL from the viewpoint of world history. Terrorism must not be tolerated, of course—but this book is a precious source to see ISIL in an objective and impartial way.

For a complete list of books, visit okawabooks.com

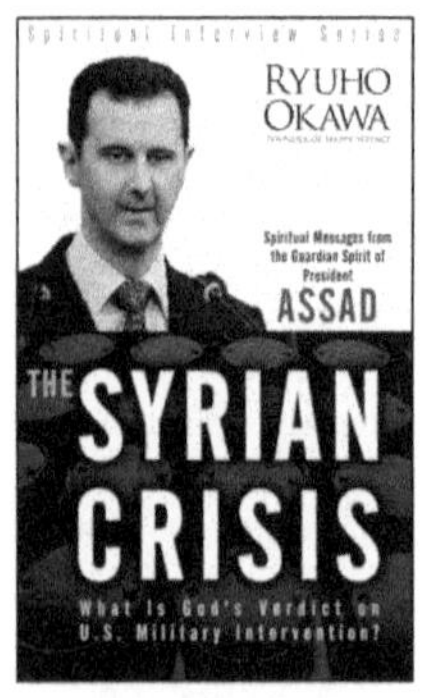

The Syrian Crisis

What Is God's Verdict on U.S. Military Intervention?

As this interview reveals, the Syrian dictator's true character is quite different from what we saw in the CBS interview. As the world braces for a possible world war, Master Ryuho Okawa provides us with a clear sense of where God's justice lies in this international crisis.

China's Secret Military Bases

A Remote-Viewing Investigation of Suspicious Satellite Images

Master Okawa reveals China's versions of Area 51 from mysterious satellite photos that had aroused worldwide curiosity. Even American intelligence will be shocked to find out these truths about a hidden enormous missile-launching site full of nuclear warheads prepared to strike major cities around the world.

South Korea's Conspiracy

President Park's Hidden Agenda to Unite with China

In this spiritual interview, we begin by speaking with the spirit of An Jung-geun before moving on to a conversation with the guardian spirit of President Park, who forced herself into the interview out of fear that the interview will reveal the truth about him. Master Okawa hopes that by revealing the truth, these interviews will help the international community understand the nature of true international justice.

For a complete list of books, visit okawabooks.com

EXPOSING NORTH KOREA'S MENACING LEADER

KIM JONG UN'S PLOT FOR A PSYCHOLOGICAL WAR

This book reveals the role that North Korea is playing in China's imperialistic strategy and the two nations' close ties with Iran. Together, China and Kim Jong Un are carrying out a psychological war that takes full advantage of the weaknesses of Japanese Prime Minister Abe and United States President Obama.

WHY I AM ANTI-JAPAN

INTERVIEWING THE GUARDIAN SPIRIT OF KOREAN PRESIDENT PARK GEUN-HYE

This book is the record of interviews conducted on President Park's subconscious [guardian spirit] in February 2014. Her true thoughts, as well as the truth on modern Japan-Korea history, were revealed in these interviews. By having numerous people in the world know of this truth, the path to create a constructive future of the Pacific Basin should open as we resolve the conflicting emotions between Japan and South Korea in the international society.

A WARNING TO SOUTH KOREA'S PRESIDENT

WORDS FROM HER FATHER, FORMER PRESIDENT PARK CHUNG-HEE

In this spiritual interview, Park Chung-hee's spirit shares his opinions on the roles of South Korea, Japan, the United States, China, and North Korea in the global context. This is a father's message to his daughter as he seeks to guide their nation in the right direction. This interview lets us see history in a new light and shows us how to build a better future for the Asia-Pacific region.

For a complete list of books, visit okawabooks.com

The Truth About WWII

Justice Pal Speaks on the Tokyo Trials

Almost 70 years ago, the Allied nations in WWII held the International Military Tribunal for the Far East [a.k.a. the Tokyo Trials] from 1946 to 1948. The book examines, in the court of spiritual history, whether the Tokyo Trials were impartial and whether Justice Pal's decision was a mistake, considering the last 70 years of modern history.

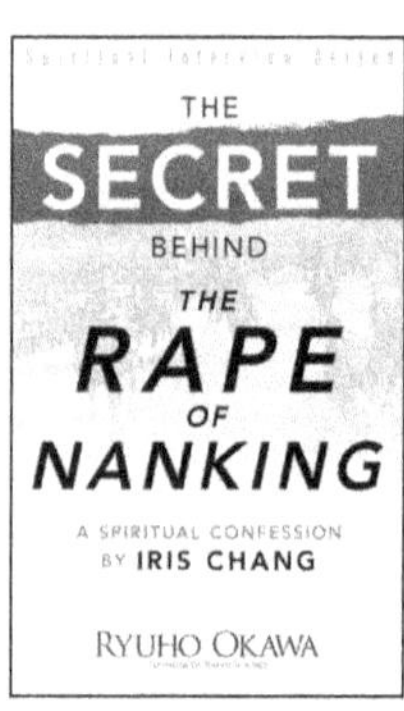

The Secret Behind "The Rape Of Nanking"

A Spiritual Confession by Iris Chang

The spirit of Iris Chang, author of a book which gave a great impact on the historical view that had spread throughout the international society today, confessed the truth regarding the content of her book and its background, just 10 years after her death, in a form of a spiritual message.

The Truth Of Nanking and Comfort Women Issues

A Spiritual Reading into World War II by Edgar Cayce

In this book, we attempt to investigate whether the two events actually took place by using a new method. This is not merely to restore the international honor of Japan. We are hoping to review the causes of World War II, look over the world justice made by the victorious nations after the war and reveal the true world history.

For a complete list of books, visit okawabooks.com

What Really Happened in Nanking?

A Spiritual Testimony of the Honorable Japanese Commander Iwane Matsui

"This book is a spiritual interview with General Iwane Matsui, who was the commanding officer during the Battle of Nanking. Will we give in to the extortion by the mere ex-prostitutes, toward the Japanese government, in their 90s who are claiming that they were military comfort women? Will we give Xi Jinping a reason for his imperialist invasion policy of the 21st century?" -From Preface

The Battle of Iwo Jima

A Memoir of Japanese General Tadamichi Kuribayashi

"I believe that offering *The Battle of Iwo Jima: A Memoir of Japanese General Tadamichi Kuribayashi* to the world will finally draw a line, 70 years after the end of WWII... I believe Japan and the U.S. should not have been enemies, but instead friends." -From Afterword

For the Love of the Country

Untold Story of the Battle of Peleliu: A Memoir of Japanese Colonel Kunio Nakagawa

"If the most intense decisive battle between Japan and the U.S. on Peleliu Island had been covered accurately and impartially by the U.S. media during WWII... we can speculate that the Korean War, the Vietnam War and even the Iraq War may not have happened." -From Preface

---

For a complete list of books, visit okawabooks.com

UNMASKING BAN KI-MOON'S BIASED STANCE

INVESTIGATING THE PARALYSIS OF THE UNITED NATIONS

Can we depend on Ban Ki-moon to successfully uphold the principle of impartiality in the United Nations's role of peacemaking? In this spiritual interview, Master Okawa reveals the U.N. Secretary-General's true character and true intentions regarding his important peacemaking responsibilities.

JAPAN! REGAIN YOUR SAMURAI SPIRIT

A MESSAGE FROM THE GUARDIAN SPIRIT OF LEE TENG-HUI, FORMER PRESIDENT OF THE REPUBLIC OF CHINA

This book is the record of interviews conducted on Former President of Taiwan Lee Teng-hui's guardian spirit in February 2014. His true thoughts, as well as the truth on modern East-Asian history, were revealed in these interviews.

LEADERSHIP SECRETS OF LIU BANG

THE EMPEROR OF CHINA'S HAN DYNASTY WITH A SURPRISING CONNECTION WITH STEVEN SPIELBERG

Everyone who aspires to lead a large organization can learn from his ability to win people's hearts. You may be surprised to discover that this long-ago emperor of China is living today in the United States as one of the world's most famous film directors, Steven Spielberg.

For a complete list of books, visit okawabooks.com

THE ART OF BUSINESS REVITALIZATION

MANAGEMENT WISDOM FROM JACK WELCH, CARLOS GHOSN, AND BILL GATES

What management philosophies or secret to creating products that become global standards or human resources management and education philosophies have they drawn upon to keep their companies at the top? This book reveals the secrets to their achievements.

STEVE JOBS RETURNS WITH HIS SECRETS

BE SIMPLE, BE CRAZY

In this spiritual interview with Steve Jobs, conducted just three months after his death, Master Okawa offers us a chance to catch a glimpse into the mind of one of America's modern geniuses. What was the aesthetic philosophy behind his passionate drive to create products? What were the secrets to his creativity and the successful sales of his products?

THE SHAPE OF THINGS IN 2100

H. G. WELLS PREDICTS THE FUTURE OF THE WORLD

What does H. G. Wells see for our future today? What was the nature of the crisis and hope he predicted in his novel, *The Shape of Things to Come*? His answers to these questions reveal the importance of bringing change to our world today to build a positive future.

For a complete list of books, visit okawabooks.com

Spiritual Messages from the Guardian Spirit of Ryuho Okawa

The Divine Voice of Shakyamuni Buddha

"The final goal is to realize what you call a 'Buddhaland Utopia.' Of course, this is not an easy task. However, it is important that you keep on making efforts to get close to it, generation after generation."

— Shakyamuni Buddha, Okawa's Guardian spirit

In Love with the Sun

Spiritual Messages from Goddess Gaia

After 600 million years, people shall know the true genesis. The true story when the earth was born, the guiding concept of the earth, the mechanism of creating life on Earth. And the future that human beings has to seek, these secrets are now revealed by the spiritual message from Goddess Gaia, who supported the creation of Earth civilization by Alpha, the God of origin.

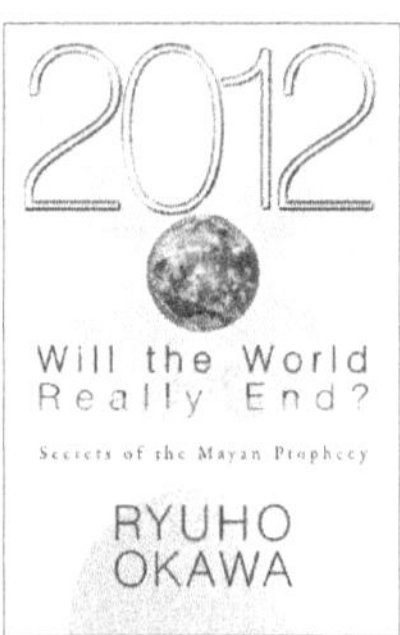

2012 Will the World Really End?

Messages from Montezuma and Quetzalcoatl

Master Okawa summoned two spirits in Heaven who are involved in the Mayan prophecy: King Montezuma of the Aztec Empire and the Mesoamerican god, Quetzalcoatl. Through these conversations, King Montezuma and Quetzalcoatl disclosed valuable hints about the spiritual secrets behind the Mayan prophecy, as well as the meaning of the major political events of 2012.

For a complete list of books, visit okawabooks.com

The Laws of Invincible Leadership

An Empowering Guide for Continuous and Lasting Success in Business and in Life

Ryuho Okawa shares essential principles for all who wish to become invincible managers and leaders in their fields of work, organizations, societies, and nations. Your keys to becoming an invincible overall winner in life and in business are just pages away.

The Laws of Great Enlightenment

Always Walk with Buddha

Constant self-blame for mistakes, setbacks, or failures and feelings of unforgivingness toward others are hard to overcome. Through the power of enlightenment we can learn to forgive ourselves and others, overcome life's problems, and courageously create a brighter future ourselves. The Laws of Great Enlightenment addresses the core problems of life that people often struggle with and offers advice on how to overcome them based on spiritual truths.

The Mystical Laws

Going Beyond the Dimensional Boundaries

"I believe that once you have finished reading this book, you will find it impossible to return to your old self, for you have now learned the secrets that run through this world and the other.

-From the Afterword

For a complete list of books, visit okawabooks.com

THE LAWS OF WISDOM

SHINE YOUR DIAMOND WITHIN

This book guides you along the path on how to acquire wisdom, so that you can break through any wall you are facing or will confront in your life or in your business. By reading this book, you will be able to avoid getting lost in the flood of information and go beyond the level of just amassing knowledge. You will be able to come up with many great ideas, make effective planning and strategy and develop your leadership while receiving good inspiration.

THE LAWS OF PERSEVERANCE

REVERSING YOUR COMMON SENSE

"No matter how much you suffer, the Truth will gradually shine forth as you continue to endure hardships. Therefore, simply strengthen your mind and keep making constant efforts in times of endurance, however ordinary they may be. "

-From Postscript

THE LAWS OF HOPE

THE LIGHT IS HERE

Learn the authentic way to realize your hopes based on the Laws of Mind. We attract what is sympathetic to our mindset. Learn the wisdom to conquer life's problems and fulfill your mission of Light. Discover how you can be the hope for the world and the future!

For a complete list of books, visit okawabooks.com

THE LAWS OF FUTURE

HERALD A NEW EARTH ERA

Fight hard for the sake of the future. You must wish, "I will open up a new future, not only for my own sake, but for God's sake, for Buddha's sake, for the sake of my fellow humans with Buddha nature, for the sake of the future of humankind, and for the sake of the world." The road to victory is open before you.

-From Prologue

[This book is available only in local branches and temples. Please refer to the contact information.]

THE LAWS OF SALVATION

FAITH AND THE FUTURE SOCIETY

Why are religions essential to us?
Why should we believe in them?
What is the goal of Happy Science?
—This book will provide you with the answers to these questions.

[This book is available only in local branches and temples. Please refer to the contact information.]

THE LAWS OF CREATION

"No Drop out of the existing "elite track" and create a new one by yourself. This is the true pleasure of life. Respect the weird and strange, and become an honorable eccentric yourself. Be a wonderful eccentric. Be courageous. Become the flag-bearer of the new civilization. Abandon your fearful heart and take on a challenge!"

-From Afterword

[This book is available only in local branches and temples. Please refer to the contact information.]

For a complete list of books, visit okawabooks.com

THE LAWS OF COURAGE

UNLEASH YOUR TRUE POTENTIAL TO OPEN A PATH FOR THE FUTURE

In a world of competition and conflict, it is easy to lose sight of who we really are and become overwhelmed by what happens around us. In this book, Ryuho Okawa presents a new perspective to discover a way to live your life with confidence and strength. This book can guide you to a new future for yourself and the world.

THE LAWS OF HAPPINESS

THE FOUR PRINCIPLES FOR A SUCCESSFUL LIFE

This is a basic introduction to the teachings of Ryuho Okawa, illustrating his core philosophy. He shows you how to free yourself from the suffering of selfish love; how to stop bemoaning your ignorance and learn through study how to cut off negative spiritual influences through self-reflection; and how your strong thoughts will be realized.

SECRETS OF THE EVERLASTING TRUTHS

A NEW PARADIGM FOR LIVING ON EARTH

In this book, Master Okawa shows us an extraordinary array of miracles that are increasing by the day. He reveals the fascinating truth that miracles occur through the help of Heaven and even space-people with whom we Earth-people have shared a very close relationship for millennia. He also shows us a glimpse of the power within knowing the existence of a vaster universe created by God.

For a complete list of books, visit okawabooks.com

Prosperity Thinking

Developing The Mindset For Attracting Infinite Riches

When you think about wealth, its starting point is to benefit more and more people. Or, put differently, being wealthy is to be appreciated by more and more people. This is the source of wealth.

-From Chapter 2

Introduction to Top Executive Management

How to Turn Every Opportunity into Success

This is a one-of-a-kind management textbook that provides you with management knowledge and teaches you a great mindset that has a close connection to the state of non-ego in Buddhism. It is a book to help top executives and top executives-to-be, who are under harsh economic conditions and who are in both commercial and non-profit organizations, turn every opportunity into success.

Thinking Financially Practical Skills of a Corporate Strategist

This book offers the essence of financial thinking that is needed in developmental stages of companies or non-profit organizations, from their launching to expanding and growing into big organizations. You'll see in this book the fundamentals of financial thinking that managers and financial experts should use to resolve their problems in everyday work.

For a complete list of books, visit okawabooks.com

THE MOMENT OF TRUTH

BECOME A LIVING ANGEL TODAY

This book shows that we are essentially spiritual beings and that our true and lasting happiness is not found within the material world but rather in acts of unconditional and selfless love toward the greater world. These pages reveal God's mind, His mercy, and His hope that many of us will become living angels that shine light onto this world.

SPIRITUAL WORLD 101

A GUIDE TO A SPIRITUALLY HAPPY LIFE

This book is a spiritual guidebook that will answer all your questions about the spiritual world,with illustrations and diagrams explaining about your guardian spirit and the secrets of God and Buddha. By reading this book, you will be able to understand the true meaning of life and find happiness in everyday life.

BASICS OF EXORCISM

HOW TO PROTECT YOU AND YOUR FAMILY FROM EVIL SPIRITS

No matter how much time progresses, demons are real. Spiritual screen against curses - the truth of exorcism as told by the author who possesses the six great supernatural powers - The essence of exorcism as a result of more than 5000 rounds of exorcist experience!

For a complete list of books, visit okawabooks.com

LEARNING THE SPIRIT OF THE FOUNDER OF HAPPY SCIENCE UNIVERSITY PART I (OVERVIEW)

WHAT IS ACADEMIC DISCIPLINE BASED ON A RELIGIOUS SPIRIT?

"The subject of this book is not just for the establishment of the university. It reveals an unwavering set of guiding principles that will serve as a "North Star" for those aspiring to live in a new era." - Excerpt from Preface

THE NEW IDEA OF A UNIVERSITY

THE GROUNDBREAKING MISSION OF HAPPY SCIENCE UNIVERSITY

In this book, the author and founder of Happy Science University, shares his vision for Happy Science University, a new type of university that has no equivalent anywhere in the world. This book opens new frontiers of academia and that provides clear guidelines for leading the world into a better future.

THE BASIC TEACHINGS OF HAPPY SCIENCE

A HAPPINESS THEORY ON TRUTH AND FAITH

When you finish reading this book, three key words, Truth, Faith and Mission that are indispensable to achieve happiness will be left in your heart, and you are bound to discover yourself filled with the wish to live a life of Truth.

For a complete list of books, visit okawabooks.com

THE TEN PRINCIPLES FROM EL CANTARE VOLUME I

RYUHO OKAWA'S FIRST LECTURES ON HIS BASIC TEACHINGS

This book contains the historic lectures given on the first five principles of the Ten Principles of Happy Science from the author, Ryuho Okawa, who is revered as World Teacher. These lectures produced an enthusiastic fellowship in Happy Science Japan and became the foundation of the current global utopian movement. You can learn the essence of Okawa's teachings and the secret behind the rapid growth of the Happy Science movement in simple language.

THE TEN PRINCIPLES FROM EL CANTARE VOLUME II

RYUHO OKAWA'S FIRST LECTURES ON HIS WISH TO SAVE THE WORLD

A sequel to *The Ten Principles from El Cantare Volume I.* Volume II reveals the Creator's three major inventions; the secret of the creation of human souls, the meaning of time, and 'happiness' as life's purpose. By reading this book, you can not only improve yourself but learn how to make differences in society and create an ideal, utopian world.

THE UNHAPPINESS SYNDROME

28 HABITS OF UNHAPPY PEOPLE (AND HOW TO CHANGE THEM)

In this book, Ryuho Okawa diagnoses the 28 common habits of the Unhappiness Syndrome and offers prescriptions for changing them so that we can cure ourselves of this syndrome. Find out whether you fall into any of the 28 patterns so that you can free yourself from worries, distress, and emotional pain. With the prescriptions offered in this book, you can start to think and act in a way that attracts happiness and open a path to a positive, bright, and happy future!

For a complete list of books, visit okawabooks.com

Healing Power

The True Mechanism of Mind and Illness

This book clearly describes the relationship between the mind and illness, and provides you with hints to restore your mental and physical health. Cancer, heart disease, allergy, skin disease, dementia, psychiatric disorder, atopy... Many miracles of healing are happening!

Miraculous Ways to Conquer Cancer

Awaken to the Power of Healing Within You

Why do people get cancer? Why does the number of patients with cancer keep increasing in spite of medical progress? This book reveals how the mind creates cancer and the keys to overcome illnesses. Drive out cancer from your life!

Healing from Within

Life-Changing Keys to Calm, Spiritual, and Healthy Living

None of us wants to become sick, but why is it that we can't avoid illness in life? Is there a meaning behind illness? In this book, author Ryuho Okawa reveals the true causes and remedies for various illnesses that modern medicine doesn't know how to heal. Building a happier and healthier life starts with believing in the power of our mind and understanding the relationship between mind and body.

For a complete list of books, visit okawabooks.com

Tips to Find Happiness

Creating a Harmonious Home for Your Spouse, Your Children, and Yourself

This is a series of questions and answers on common problems in marriage, work, and relationships, offering a wide range of both practical and spiritual suggestions that will be sure to resonate with everyone who has experienced difficulties in the home.

Guideposts to Happiness

Prescriptions for a Wonderful Life

In this book, author and spiritual leader Ryuho Okawa describes in detail some of the negative patterns of thinking that keep us from attaining peace of mind. He outlines the causes of a number of life's problems, including depression, inferiority complexes and conflicts that result from over-assertiveness. In this book, you will find many hints to help you solve your worries and attain true happiness.

The Origin of Love

On the Beauty of Compassion

Why do people love each other, or hate each other? In this book, spiritual teacher Ryuho Okawa answers this question by referring to the origin of love in relation to the secret of eternal life. When you understand the Truth about love, you will be awakened to the wonder of being given life, and you will be filled with love for those around you.

For a complete list of books, visit okawabooks.com

The Starting Point of Happiness

An Inspiring Guide to Positive Living with Faith, Love, and Courage

In this book, Ryuho Okawa awakens us to the true spiritual values of our life; he beautifully illustrates, in simple but profound words, how we can find purpose and meaning in life and attain happiness that lasts forever. This self-renewing guide to positive living will awaken us to the spiritual truths, infuse us with hope, strength and fulfillment, and lead us to walk the path to authentic, lasting happiness.

Love, Nurture, and Forgive

A Handbook to Add a New Richness to Your Life

Master Okawa reveals the secrets of spiritual growth based on his own real life experiences. Starting from practicing the "love that gives," instead of expecting something in return for what you have done to help others, you can experience a remarkable transformation through your own self help efforts to develop through the stages of love.

Invincible Thinking

An Essential Guide for a Lifetime of Growth, Success, and Triumph

In this book, Ryuho Okawa lays out the principles of invincible thinking that will allow us to achieve long-lasting triumph. This powerful and unique philosophy is not only about becoming successful or achieving our goal in life, but also about building the foundation of life that becomes the basis of our life-long, lasting success and happiness.

For a complete list of books, visit okawabooks.com

THE PHILOSOPHY OF PROGRESS

HIGHER THINKING FOR DEVELOPING INFINITE PROSPERITY

What is wealth? Is money good or evil? These have been controversial issues and no one ever seems to have answered these simple questions clearly. In this book, Ryuho Okawa provides us with answers on wealth, prosperity, and progress from a perspective based on spiritual truth. He teaches that as long as people hold on to poverty in their minds, they will never become wealthy.

AN UNSHAKABLE MIND

HOW TO OVERCOME LIFE'S DIFFICULTIES

This book describes ways to build inner confidence and achieve spiritual growth, adopting a spiritual perspective as the basis. With a willingness to learn from everything that life presents you, good or bad, any difficulty can be transformed into nourishment for the soul.

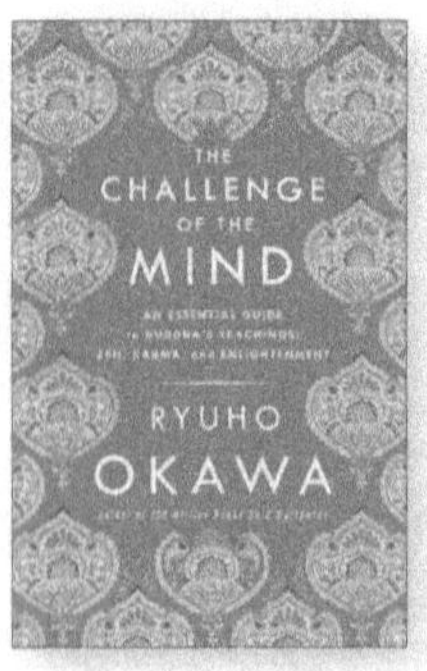

THE CHALLENGE OF THE MIND

AN ESSENTIAL GUIDE TO BUDDHA'S TEACHINGS: ZEN, KARMA AND ENLIGHTENMENT

In this book, Ryuho Okawa explains essential Buddhist tenets and how to put them into practice. Enlightenment is not just an abstract idea but one that everyone can experience to some extent. Okawa offers a solid basis of reason and intellectual understanding to Buddhist concepts. By applying these basic principles to our lives, we can direct our minds to higher ideals and create a bright future for ourselves and others.

For a complete list of books, visit okawabooks.com

The Essence of Buddha

The Path to Enlightenment

This book is about living a life with meaning and purpose. It offers a contemporary interpretation of the way to enlightenment, written by highly revered spiritual leader. The fundamental tenets of the Buddhist understanding of life, such as The Eightfold Path, The Six Paramitas and the Laws of Causality, are clearly explained in modern and accessible terms, along with the need for self-reflection, the nature of karma and reincarnation, and other teachings of the Buddha. Enlightenment is a potential achievement for every sentient being

The Rebirth of Buddha

My Eternal Disciples, Hear My Words

These are the messages of Buddha who has returned to this modern age as promised to His eternal beloved disciples. They are in simple words and poetic style, yet contain profound messages. Once you start reading these passages, your soul will be replenished as the plant absorbs the water, and you will remember why you chose this era to be born into with Buddha. Listen to the voices of your Eternal Master and awaken to your calling.

The Eternal Buddha

"The Laws of Eternal Buddha flow swiftly like the waters of the Ganges River as it merges eternal mystery with clear logic. That which was Truth 2,500 years ago, is Truth today, and will remain as Truth 3,000 years from now. For this reason, they are the most victorious of all teachings. "
-From Preface

[This book is available only in local branches and temples. Please refer to the contact information.]

For a complete list of books, visit okawabooks.com

Messages From Heaven

What Jesus, Buddha, Muhammad, and Moses Would Say Today

If you could speak to Jesus, Buddha, Moses, or Muhammad, what would you ask? In this book, Ryuho Okawa shares the spiritual communication he had with these four spirits and the messages they want to share with people living today. The Truths revealed in this book will open your eyes to a level of spiritual awareness, salvation, and happiness that you have never experienced before.

Think Big!

Be Positive and Be Brave to Achieve Your Dreams

Think Big! offers the support and encouragement to shift to new ways of thinking and mastering self-discipline. Okawa's self-proven approach fosters stability and strength in the challenges each of us faces. In addition to his relatable stories and a motivational voice to keep us going, each chapter builds on the next for concrete methodologies that, when added up, are a track to support your dreams, yourself, and your life.

The Heart of Work

10 Keys to Living Your Calling

In this book, Ryuho Okawa shares 10 key philosophies and goals to live by to guide us through our work lives and triumphantly live our calling. There are key principles that will help you get to the heart of work, manage your time well, prioritize your work, live with long health and vitality, achieve growth, and more.

www.ingramcontent.com/pod-product-compliance
Lightning Source LLC
Chambersburg PA
CBHW032100020426
42335CB00011B/434